WE STAND WITH UKRAINE

ONE EQUALS MANY

SONNY DEAN

LITTLE LAMBDA

BOOKS

www.LittleLambdaBooks.com

Ще не вмерла України і слава, і воля,
Ще нам, браття молодії, усміхнеться доля.
Згинуть наші воріженьки, як роса на сонці.
Запануєм і ми, браття, у своїй сторонці.

Душу й тіло ми положим за нашу свободу,
І покажем, що ми, браття, козацького роду.

-Державний Гімн України

The glory and freedom of Ukraine has not yet perished,
Upon us, my young brothers, fate shall yet smile.
Our enemies will perish like dew in the sun.
And we too shall reign, brothers, in our own land.

We will lay down our souls and bodies for our freedom,
And we will show that we, brothers, are of the Cossack family.

-National Anthem of Ukraine

One pebble

may seem

small...

Together, pebbles
make the
Carpathian Mountains.

One drop
of water
may seem
small...

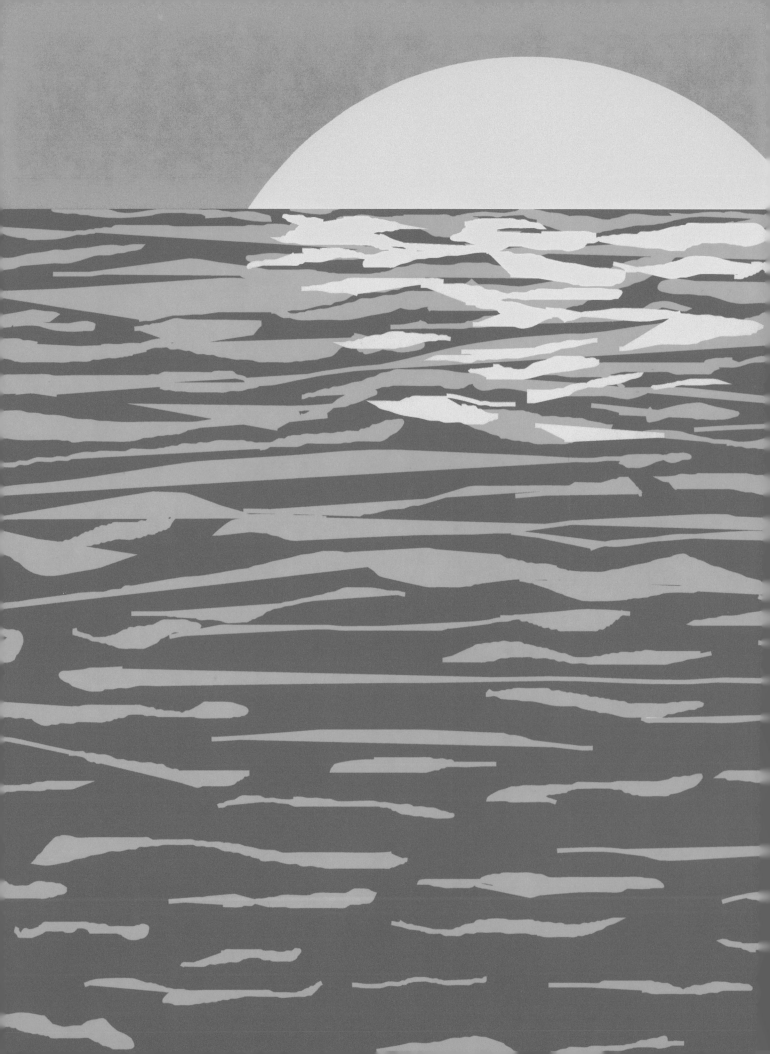

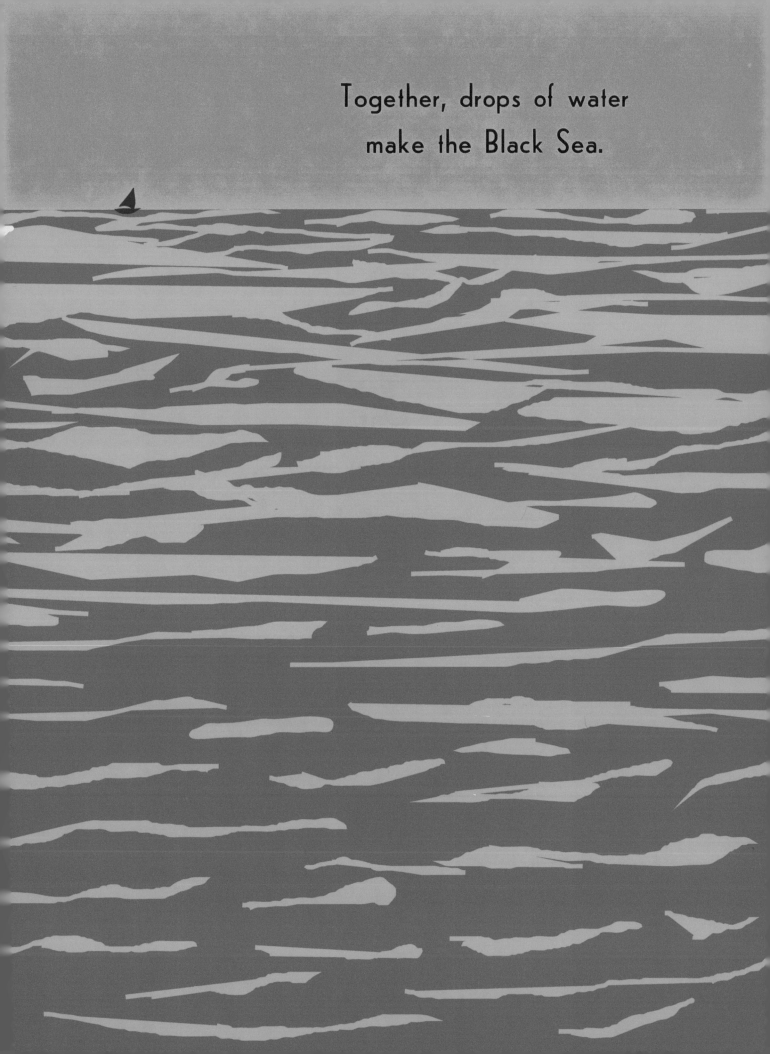

Together, drops of water
make the Black Sea.

One
musical note
may seem
small...

Together, notes make the National Anthem of Ukraine.

One letter

may seem

small...

A

Together, letters tell the stories of a proud history and glorious culture that cannot be extinguished.

One step

may seem

small...

Together, steps make
a journey to safety.

And a journey home.

One pine cone

may seem

small...

Together, pine cones make
the Cherkasy Forest.

One vote
may seem
small...

BALLOT

 Oppression

 Freedom

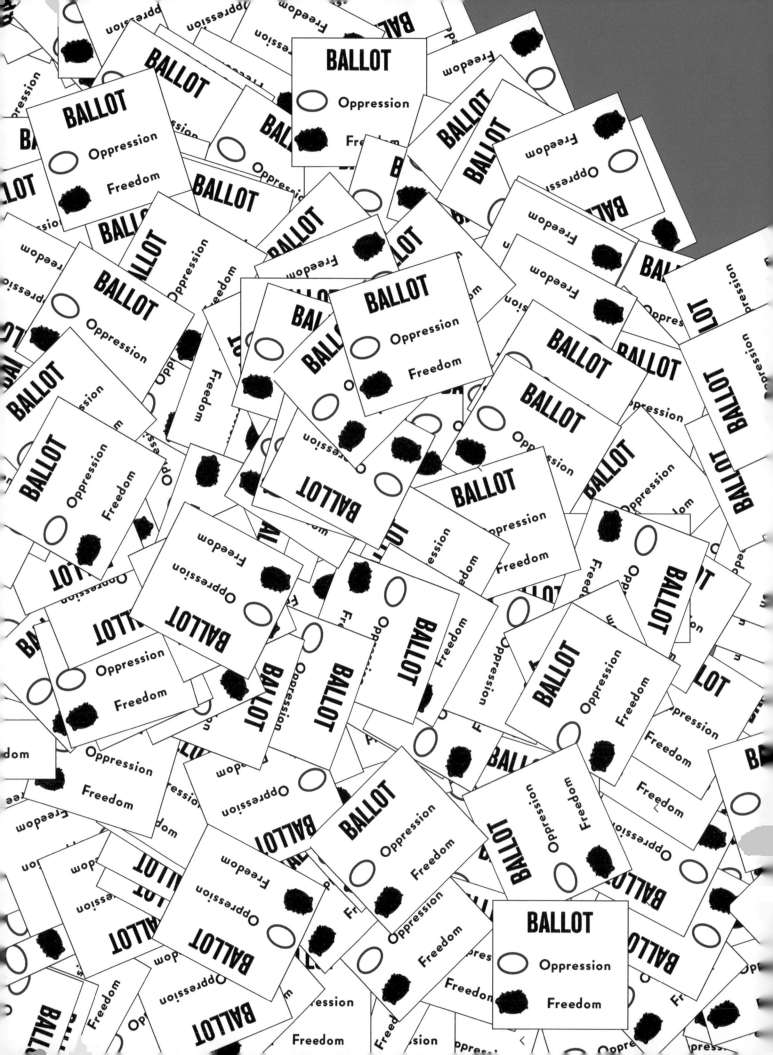

Together, votes make a landslide.

Every single one of us can do our part to help, by calling our elected officials and urging action, raising money for relief efforts, fighting disinformation, and voting into power those who will do the right thing.

And...

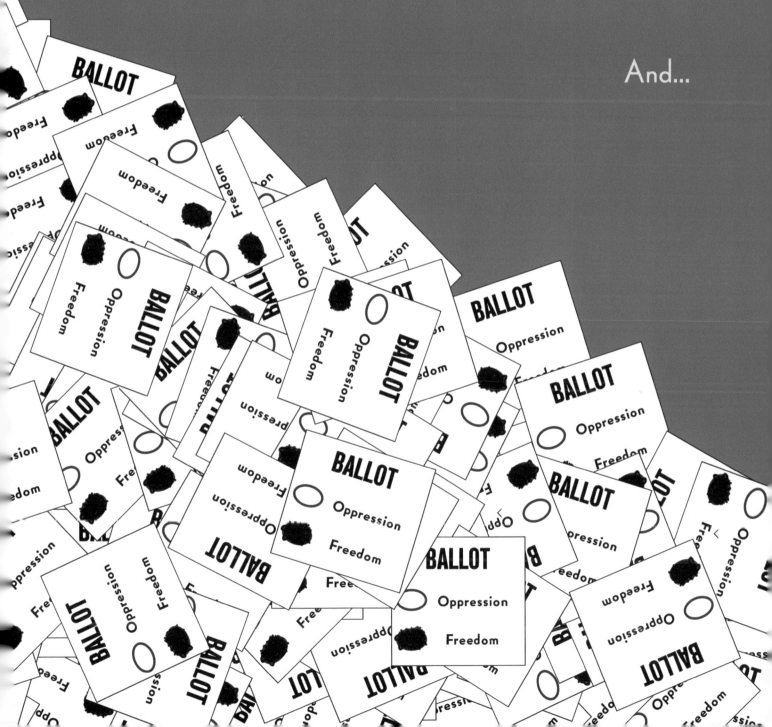

That can
change the world.

Hardcover ISBN: 978-1-958194-00-3
2 4 6 8 10 9 7 5 3 1

Ebook ISBN: 978-1-958194-01-0
Paperback ISBN: 978-1-7344663-8-6
Library of Congress Cataloging-in-Publication Data is available.

LITTLE LAMBDA

BOOKS LLC

www.LittleLambdaBooks.com

The publisher and author are donating
all of their profits from the sale of this book to
the United Nations Crisis Relief efforts in Ukraine:

https://crisisrelief.un.org

Show us how you are helping!

The blank pages in this book are for you to
draw a picture or write a story about how
you are making the world a better place.
Send us a picture! We'd love to see it!

About Little Lambda Books:

Little Lambda Books is a small Maine publishing company founded in 2019, with a mission to
make the world a better place by publishing stories that matter. We founded our company when
we saw a need for a niche publishing house that would develop substantive children's books that
promote respect and kindness, tackle tough subjects that are too often avoided, and have
more than a nominal commitment to give back to our community. We strongly believe that
each of us can and must do our part to make our world a more caring and just place.

Facebook & Instagram: @LittleLambdaBooks

About the Author and Illustrator:

Sonny lives in Maine in a cozy cottage by the sea, surrounded by a forest filled with an
astonishing assortment of interesting creatures. She fled a successful career in corporate
marketing to tell the stories that she would have liked to have read as a child.
When she is not writing or drawing (or daydreaming), she can be found enjoying nature with
her family, exploring museums, or curled up on her window seat with a towering heap of good books.

Facebook & Instagram: @TheSonnyDean

Books by Sonny Dean:

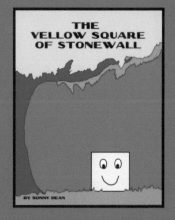

CPSIA information can be obtained
at www.ICGtesting.com
Printed in the USA
BVHW021741240822
645432BV00008B/134